100 facts
Gladiators

Rupert Matthews

Consultant: Philip Steele

Miles Kelly

First published as hardback in 2005 by Miles Kelly Publishing Ltd
Bardfield Centre, Great Bardfield, Essex, CM7 4SL

This edition printed in 2009

2 4 6 8 10 9 7 5 3

Editorial Director: Belinda Gallagher
Art Director: Jo Brewer
Project Manager: Lisa Clayden
Assistant Editor: Lucy Dowling
Volume Designer: Louisa Leitao
Picture Researcher: Jennifer Hunt
Copy Editor: Kate Lodge
Proofreader: Margaret Berrill
Indexer: Jane Parker
Production Manager: Elizabeth Brunwin
Reprographics: Anthony Cambray, Stephan Davis,
Jennifer Hunt, Liberty Newton, Ian Paulyn
Editions Manager: Bethan Ellish

ISBN 978-1-84236-878-7

Printed in China

British Library Cataloguing-in-Publication Data
A catalogue record for this book is available from the British Library

ACKNOWLEDGEMENTS
Cover artwork by Andrea Morandi

The publishers would like to thank the following
sources for the use of their photographs:

Page 6 Bettmann/Corbis; 14 Bettmann/Corbis;
42 Roger Wood/Corbis; 43 Dreamworks/Universal/Pictorial Press;
44 K M Westermann/Corbis; 45 Bryna/Universal/Pictorial Press;
46 Dreamworks/Universal/Pictorial Press

All other images from the Miles Kelly Archives

Made with paper from a sustainable forest

www.mileskelly.net
info@mileskelly.net

www.factsforprojects.com
The one-stop homework helper — pictures, facts, videos, projects and more

Contents

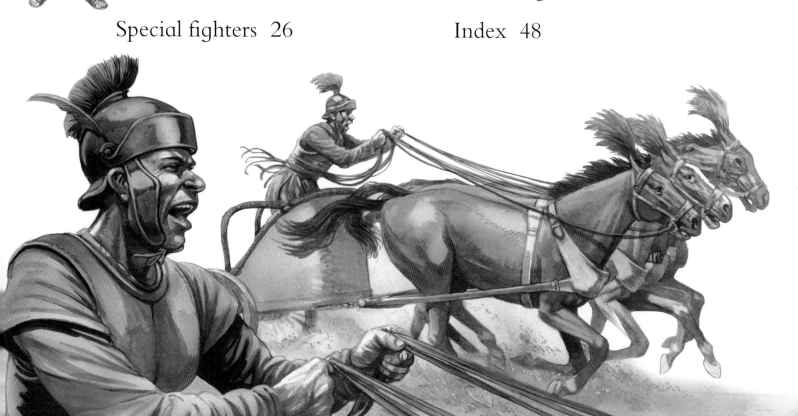

The great games

1 Gladiators were made to fight to the death to please the crowd. They fought in an arena (open space surrounded by tiered seats) and used lots of different swords, spears, knives and other weapons. Not every gladiatorial fight ended in death. Some gladiators were allowed to live if they fought bravely and with skill. Most fights took place in Rome, but cities throughout the Roman Empire had arenas for these events. The arenas were also used for wild animal hunts and for the execution of criminals. For the ancient Romans, violence and bloodshed were used as entertainment.

▶ A defeated gladiator appeals for mercy from the crowd by raising his left hand. The victorious fighter awaits the instruction to kill or spare his rival.

The first gladiators

2 **The first gladiators were not from Rome.** The Romans did not invent the idea of gladiators. They believed the idea of men fighting in an arena probably came to Rome from the region of Etruria. But the first proper gladiators probably came from Campania, an area of Italy south of Rome.

▲ The city of Rome began as a small town between Etruria and Campania in central Italy.

QUIZ

1. What were the gladiators named after?
2. Did the Romans invent the idea of gladiators?
3. What word did the Romans use to describe a gladiator show?

Answers:
1. Gladiators were named after the gladius, a type of short sword. 2. No. The idea came from the people of Campania, an area to the south of Rome. 3. The Romans called a gladiator show a munus.

3 **The first Roman gladiators fought in 264BC.** Six slaves were set to fight each other with swords, but they were not allowed to wear any armour. The fights did not last long before one of the slaves in each pair was killed.

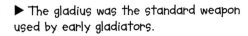

▶ The gladius was the standard weapon used by early gladiators.

4 **The first gladiatorial fights were always part of a funeral.** The name for a gladiatorial show, a munus, means a duty owed to the dead. The first fights were held at the funerals of politicians and noblemen, who ordered the games in their wills.

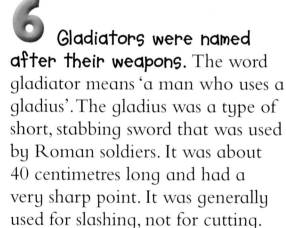

▶ The first gladiators were usually elderly slaves or troublemakers, who would not be missed much by their owners.

5 **In early funeral games, food was more important than gladiators.** The Romans used funerals to show off how wealthy and important they were. Free food and drink were laid out at the funeral for any Roman citizen who wanted to come along. Gifts of money, jewellery and clothing were also handed out. The family of the person being buried would wear their finest clothes. The first gladiator fights were just one part of the whole funeral.

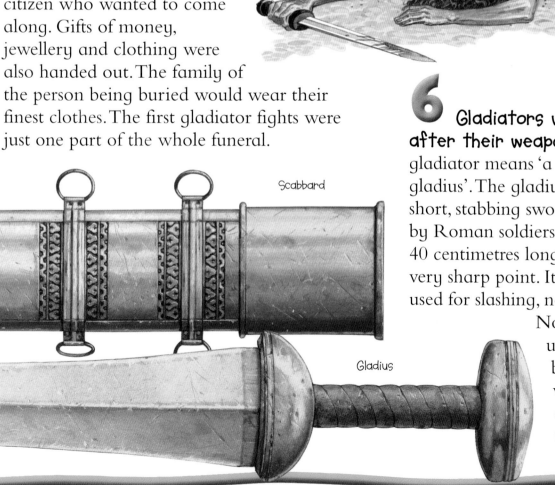

Scabbard

Gladius

6 **Gladiators were named after their weapons.** The word gladiator means 'a man who uses a gladius'. The gladius was a type of short, stabbing sword that was used by Roman soldiers. It was about 40 centimetres long and had a very sharp point. It was generally used for slashing, not for cutting.

Not all gladiators used the gladius, but the name was used for all fighters in the arena.

Prisoners of war

▼ A Thracian armed with a square shield and curved sword faces a Samnite equipped with a larger shield and longer, straight sword.

Samnite

Thracian

7 **Prisoners of war fought in the arena.** Between 250BC and 100BC the Romans fought many wars against foreign enemies. Prisoners captured in these wars were sold as slaves in Rome. Captured soldiers were made to fight in the arena, with weapons and armour from their own country.

8 **The Samnites had the best weapons.** The Romans fought a long series of wars against the Samnites between 343BC and 290BC. These men each carried a large, oval shield and wore a helmet with cheek guards (flaps that protected their cheeks). Samnite gladiators were famous for the quality of their swords and spears.

9 **The Thracians had the strangest weapons.** The men from the kingdom of Thrace carried small shields and wore helmets with crests. They were famous for being able to hit any target with their spears and carried short, curved swords. This mix of weapons proved very popular and many gladiators adopted them. They became known as Thracian gladiators, even if they were not from Thrace.

I DON'T BELIEVE IT!

At the end of a war the prisoners were auctioned as slaves in the Forum (market square). Sometimes so many prisoners had been taken that the auction lasted for many days.

▶ The tall, fair-skinned Celts decorated their bodies and shields with bright colours.

10 **Celts painted their bodies before going into battle.** The Celts were the only people to have captured Rome, in 390 BC. They lived in northern Italy and across Europe. The Romans forced many Celtic prisoners to fight in their native clothes and with native weapons.

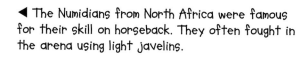

◀ The Numidians from North Africa were famous for their skill on horseback. They often fought in the arena using light javelins.

11 **The Numidians fought on horseback.** Numidia was an area of northern Africa in what is now Algeria. The area was famous for breeding quality horses and its army included large numbers of cavalry (soldiers on horseback). Prisoners of war from Numidia rode horses when they appeared in the arena.

Gladiators and politics

▲ A person's ashes were stored in a pot or urn until the funeral.

12 Funerals were delayed for years. Gladiatorial shows were organized as part of the funerals of rich and powerful noblemen. However, the heir of the man who had died would want to hold the show when he was standing for election so that he could impress the voters.

13 A good gladiator show could win an election. In ancient Rome, votes were not cast in secret. Each voter had to give his name to an official called a censor and then declare how he was voting. The men standing for election stood near the censor to see how people voted. Putting on an impressive gladiator show could gain votes.

▼ A citizen waiting to vote at an election. The censor kept a list of everyone entitled to vote and people had to prove who they were before voting.

I DON'T BELIEVE IT!

In 165BC, a play was interrupted when the entire audience left the theatre to watch a gladiatorial show. All the actors were left alone in the theatre!

14 Some politicians hired gangs of gladiators to beat up their opponents. If a citizen could not be persuaded, by gladiator shows or the payment of money, to vote for a certain candidate, the candidate might use gladiators to bully him. Gladiators were armed with clubs and given the names of citizens who should be threatened. Every election was accompanied by this sort of violence.

▲ Men were posted at the entrance to the arena to ensure that only voters entered.

15 Only voters could watch the games. The purpose of holding spectacular gladiatorial shows was to influence voters. Only citizens of Rome could vote, so only they were allowed to attend the shows. Citizens who were known to be voting for an opponent were turned away, as were slaves and foreigners who could not vote.

16 The best seats went to men who donated money to the election campaign. Standing for an election cost a lot of money in ancient Rome. Rich men would give or lend money to the candidate they preferred. In return they would get the best seats in a gladiatorial show and would expect to receive titles or government money if their candidate won.

◀ Roman coins were made of gold, silver or bronze and carried a portrait of the emperor on one side.

Spartacus!

17 The most famous gladiator of all was Spartacus. He led a rebellion of gladiators and other slaves in the year 73BC. At first Spartacus had just 70 gladiators with him, but later over 40,000 runaway slaves joined his forces.

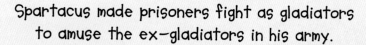
18 Spartacus was a gladiator from the kingdom of Thrace. He joined the Roman army, but did not like it and tried to run away. As a punishment, Spartacus was sent to train as a gladiator, although he was allowed to take his wife with him.

19 The gladiators, led by Spartacus, defeated the Roman army. After breaking out of the gladiator school (called a ludus), Spartacus hid on the slopes of Mount Vesuvius, near Naples. He defeated a small Roman force sent to capture him and then led his growing army to northern Italy. There, at Modena, he defeated a large Roman army and stole valuable goods.

20 Spartacus wanted to cross the Alps, a large mountain range. After winning the battle at Modena, Spartacus wanted to return to Thrace. However, his men wanted to raid cities. They made Spartacus lead them back to southern Italy.

21 The wrong general was credited for defeating Spartacus. Spartacus and his army of slaves and gladiators were defeated by a new Roman army at Lucania. This army was commanded by Marcus Licinius Crassus. One small group of slaves fled the battle and was captured by a commander named Gnaeus Pompey. He then rode to Rome and announced that he had defeated the rebels.

◄ The 1960 movie *Spartacus* starred Kirk Douglas (centre) as the escaped gladiator. Spartacus equipped his army of gladiators and slaves with weapons stolen from the Romans.

Caesar's games

22 **Julius Caesar borrowed money to buy his gladiators.** Julius Caesar rose to become the ruler of the Roman Empire. Early in his career he staged spectacular games to win votes in elections. But Caesar was too poor to afford to pay the bills, so he borrowed money from richer men. When he won the elections, Caesar repaid the men with favours and titles.

▲ Julius Caesar (102–44BC) was a politician who won several elections after staging magnificent games to entertain the voters.

▼ War elephants were popular attractions, and gladiators were specially trained in how to fight against them.

23 **Caesar's gladiators fought in silver armour.** In 65BC, Julius Caesar staged the funeral games for his father, who had died 20 years earlier. Caesar was standing for election to be chief priest of Rome. To make his games even more special, Caesar dressed his 640 gladiators in armour made of solid silver.

24 **Caesar brought war elephants to Rome.** In 46BC Julius Caesar celebrated a victory in North Africa by staging gladiatorial games in Rome. Among the prisoners of war forced to fight in the arena were 40 war elephants, together with the men trained to fight them.

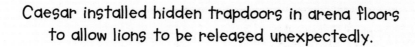
25

Caesar turned senators (governors of Rome) into gladiators. On one occasion Caesar forced two rich noblemen to fight in the arena. They had been sentenced to death by a court, but Caesar ordered that the man who killed the other in the arena could go free.

26

Caesar's final show was too big for the arena. The games staged by Julius Caesar when he wanted to become dictator of Rome were the grandest ever held. After weeks of shows and feasts, the final day saw a fight between two armies of 500 infantry (foot soldiers) and 30 cavalry. The battle was so large it had to be held in the enormous chariot race course, Circus Maximus.

QUIZ

1. Did Caesar's gladiators wear armour made of silver, gold or bronze?
2. Was Caesar's final show a big or small show?
3. Where did Caesar get the money to buy gladiators?

Answers:
1. Silver. 2. It was a big show.
3. He borrowed money from richer men.

▼ Chariot racing was a hugely popular sport that thrilled the crowds in ancient Rome.

The mob

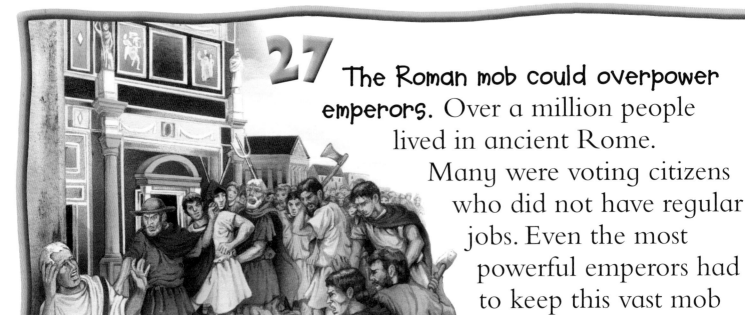

27 **The Roman mob could overpower emperors.** Over a million people lived in ancient Rome. Many were voting citizens who did not have regular jobs. Even the most powerful emperors had to keep this vast mob of Romans happy. If an emperor did not put on impressive gladiatorial shows he could be booed, attacked or even be killed.

▲ Emperor Vitellius (AD69) was murdered by a mob of Romans after failing to put on any impressive games.

▼ The seats in the arena were numbered and cushions were sometimes provided for extra comfort.

28 **Each seat was saved for a particular person.** People attending the gladiator games had their own seats. The row and seat number were written on small clay tablets that were handed out by the organizer of the games. Some seats were given to whoever queued up outside the arena.

29 Women in ancient Rome could not vote, so they were given seats at the back of the crowd. The best seats were reserved for the men who could vote and had money to help the editor (the man who staged gladiatorial games).

◄ A wounded gladiator pleads for his life by raising the first finger of his left hand. The thumbs downward signal from the mob indicates that he should die.

30 The mob decided which gladiators lived, and which died. A wounded gladiator could appeal for mercy by holding up the first finger of his left hand. The mob gave a thumbs down gesture if they thought the gladiator should die, or hid their thumbs in clenched fists if they thought he should live. The editor usually did what the mob wanted because he wanted them to vote for him.

I DON'T BELIEVE IT!
Poor Roman citizens were given free bread by the government. In one month in 44BC, over 330,000 men queued up to receive this free handout of food.

Amazing arenas

31 The first gladiator fights took place in the cattle market. The cattle market, or Forum Boarium, was a large open space by the river Tiber. Cattle pens were cleared away to make space for fighting, while the audience watched from shops and temples.

◄ The crowd watched early gladiatorial fights in the cattle market from shops and pavements.

32 Most fights took place in the Forum. This was the largest open square in the centre of Rome. The most important temples and government buildings stood around the Forum. After about 150BC, gladiatorial games were held in the Forum and temporary wooden stands were erected in which spectators could sit.

33 One fight took place in a swivelling arena. In 53BC, the politician Gaius Scribonius Curio put on a gladiator show and impressed the crowd by staging two plays in back-to-back theatres. The theatres swivelled around to form an arena for a small gladiator show. The crowd loved the new idea and Curio went on to win several elections.

34

The first purpose–built arena had the wrong name carved on it. In 29BC an amphitheatre (an open-air building with rows of seats, one above the other) was built to the north of Rome by the politician Titus Statilius Taurus. The amphitheatre was built of stone and timber to replace temporary wooden stands in the Forum. Taurus wanted to impress Emperor Augustus so he carved the name 'Augustus' over the entrance.

▼ The name Augustus dominated the entrance to the arena built by Taurus.

35

Every arena had the same layout. Arenas were oval with an entrance at each end. The gladiators came into the arena through one entrance, and the other was reserved for servants and for carrying out any dead gladiators. The editor sat in a special section of the seating called the tribunal editoris, which was on the north side in the shade.

TRUE OR FALSE?

1. The cattle market was the largest open space in Rome.
2. At first spectators watched from shops and temples.
3. Some arenas were round, some oval and some square.

Answers:
1. FALSE The Forum was the largest open space in Rome.
2. TRUE Early gladiatorial fights took place in the cattle market and spectators watched from nearby buildings. 3. FALSE All arenas were oval.

▼ All gladiatorial stadiums were oval in shape, with blocks of seating rising from the central arena.

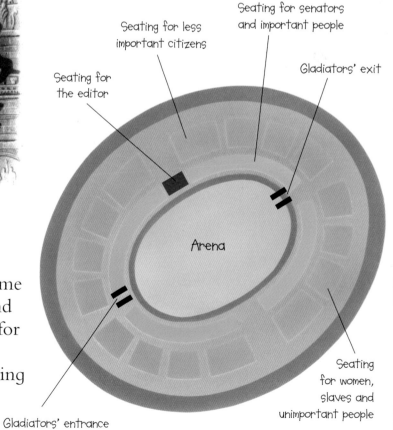

Seating for less important citizens

Seating for senators and important people

Seating for the editor

Gladiators' exit

Arena

Seating for women, slaves and unimportant people

Gladiators' entrance

The mighty Colosseum

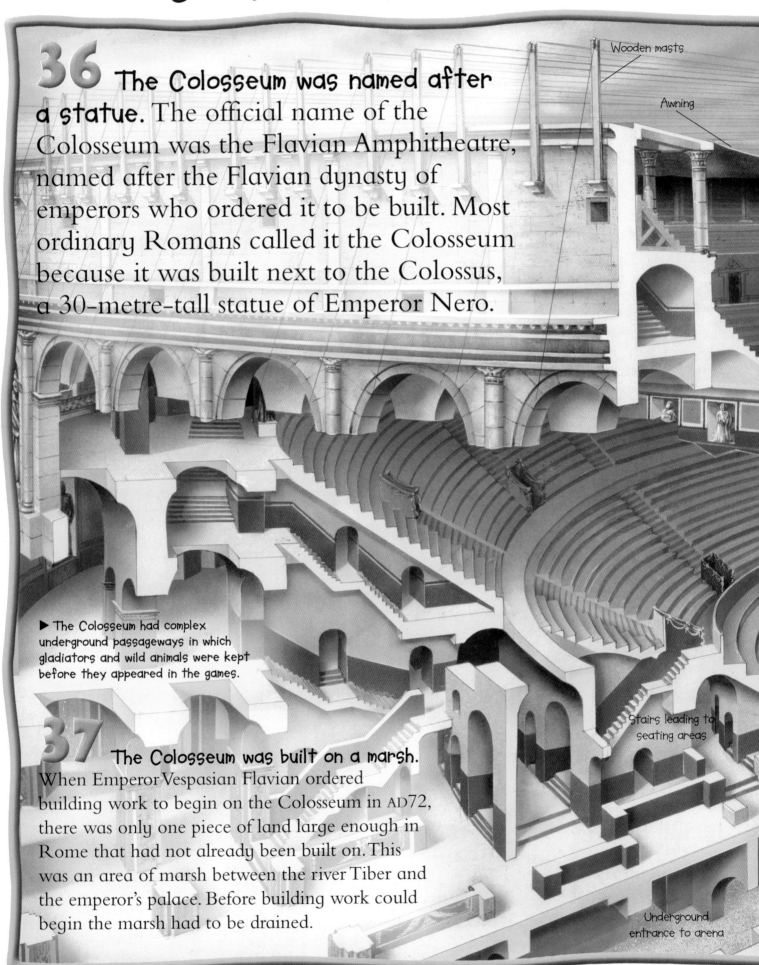

36 **The Colosseum was named after a statue.** The official name of the Colosseum was the Flavian Amphitheatre, named after the Flavian dynasty of emperors who ordered it to be built. Most ordinary Romans called it the Colosseum because it was built next to the Colossus, a 30-metre-tall statue of Emperor Nero.

Wooden masts

Awning

▶ The Colosseum had complex underground passageways in which gladiators and wild animals were kept before they appeared in the games.

37 **The Colosseum was built on a marsh.** When Emperor Vespasian Flavian ordered building work to begin on the Colosseum in AD72, there was only one piece of land large enough in Rome that had not already been built on. This was an area of marsh between the river Tiber and the emperor's palace. Before building work could begin the marsh had to be drained.

Stairs leading to seating areas

Underground entrance to arena

38 **The Colosseum could seat 50,000 spectators.** The huge seating area was divided into over 80 sections. Each section had a separate door and flight of steps that led to the outside of the Colosseum. It is thought that the entire audience could have left in less than 15 minutes of the end of the show. The standing room at the top was reserved for slaves and may have held another 4000 people.

39 **The Colosseum was probably the largest building in the world.** It was finished in AD80 and the outer walls stood over 46 metres tall and covered an area 194 metres long by 160 metres wide. The walls were covered in stone, but most of the structure was made of brick or concrete.

40 **The first games in the Colosseum lasted 100 days.** The Colosseum was finished during the reign of Emperor Titus. He wanted to show that he was the most generous man ever to live in Rome, so he organized gladiatorial games to last for 100 days. Thousands of gladiators and animals fought in these games, which some people thought were the finest ever staged in Rome.

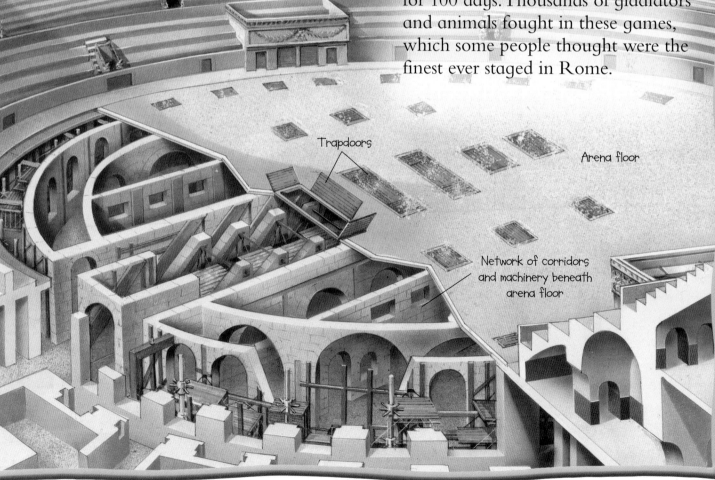

Tiered seating

Trapdoors

Arena floor

Network of corridors and machinery beneath arena floor

Who were the gladiators?

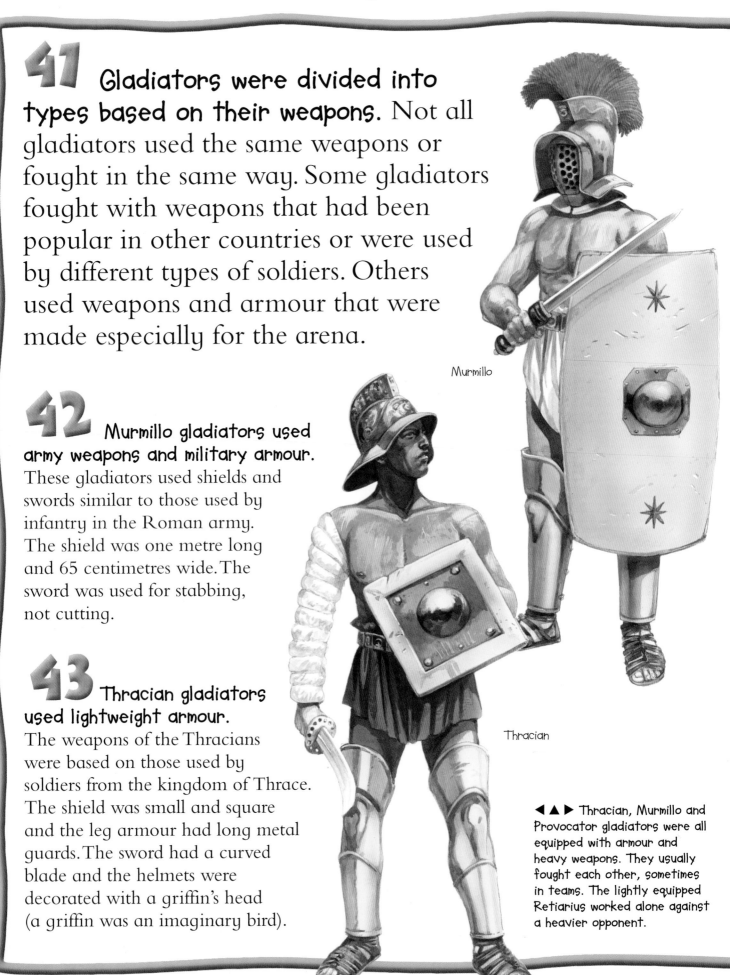

41 Gladiators were divided into types based on their weapons. Not all gladiators used the same weapons or fought in the same way. Some gladiators fought with weapons that had been popular in other countries or were used by different types of soldiers. Others used weapons and armour that were made especially for the arena.

Murmillo

42 Murmillo gladiators used army weapons and military armour. These gladiators used shields and swords similar to those used by infantry in the Roman army. The shield was one metre long and 65 centimetres wide. The sword was used for stabbing, not cutting.

43 Thracian gladiators used lightweight armour. The weapons of the Thracians were based on those used by soldiers from the kingdom of Thrace. The shield was small and square and the leg armour had long metal guards. The sword had a curved blade and the helmets were decorated with a griffin's head (a griffin was an imaginary bird).

Thracian

◀ ▲ ▶ Thracian, Murmillo and Provocator gladiators were all equipped with armour and heavy weapons. They usually fought each other, sometimes in teams. The lightly equipped Retiarius worked alone against a heavier opponent.

44 Provocator gladiators wore the heaviest armour of all gladiators. They had a breastplate that protected the chest, a round helmet and leg armour that reached above the knees. The shield was about 80 centimetres long and 60 centimetres wide. They used a short, stabbing sword with a straight blade.

Retiarius

Provocator

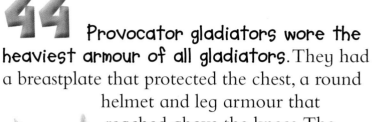

MAKE A SHIELD

You will need:
cardboard scissors
string coloured paints

1. Take the sheet of cardboard and cut out a rectangular shape with rounded corners.
2. Ask an adult to make a pair of holes close to each long side and tie string through them to make handles.
3. Paint the front of the shield with a bright, colourful design like those in this book.

45 Retiarius gladiators had a fishing net and trident. These gladiators wore very little armour. They relied on speed and skill to escape attacks from heavily equipped gladiators, such as the provocator gladiators. The fishing net was used to try to trip or entangle an opponent. The trident, a spear with three points, was usually used by fishermen.

Special fighters

◀ The equite gladiators began their combat on horseback, but if one fell off his horse, the other had to fight on foot as well.

46 **Equite gladiators were equipped in the same way as the cavalry in the Roman army.** They used a small leather shield, a medium-length sword and a lance about 2.5 metres long. Only the helmet was different from that of the army. The army helmet had an open face and no brim. Whenever these gladiators appeared in a show they were the first to fight.

47 **Female gladiators were rare.** They first appeared around AD55 in Rome as a novelty act. They fought only against other women or animals. Female gladiators were banned in AD200.

▲ Female gladiators fought in the same style as the male gladiators.

48

The andabatae (an-dab-AH-tie) fought blindfolded. The Romans loved anything new or unusual. Andabatae gladiators wore helmets with no eye-holes. They listened carefully for sounds of their opponent, then attacked with two swords. Sometimes the andabatae fought on horseback.

49

British gladiators fought from chariots. Known as the essedarii (ess-e-DAH-ree-ee), meaning chariot-man, these gladiators first appeared after Julius Caesar invaded Britain in 55BC. The first chariot gladiators were prisoners of war.

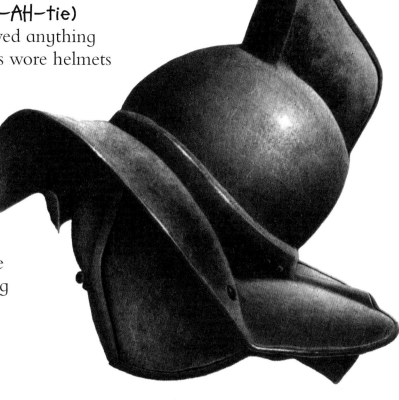

▲ Andabatae helmets had no eye-holes – the gladiators had to rely on their hearing.

ANDABATAE FIGHT

Recreate the combat of the andabatae with this game.

You will need:
blindfold four or more players

1. One player is the andabatae. Tie on the blindfold, making sure the player can see nothing.
2. Other players run around the andabatae calling out their name.
3. The andabatae tries to catch someone. When they catch a person, that person puts on the blindfold and becomes the andabatae. The game continues for as long as you like.

50

Special clowns who fought with wooden weapons were known as paegniarii (payeg-nee-AH-ree-ee). They appeared at shows during gaps between gladiator fights. They were skilled acrobats and would sometimes tell jokes or make fun of important people in the audience.

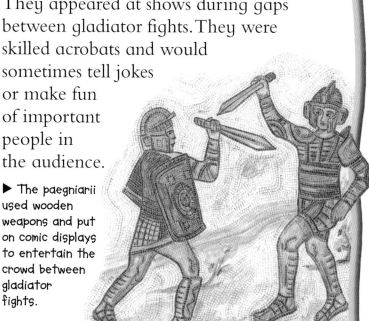

▶ The paegniarii used wooden weapons and put on comic displays to entertain the crowd between gladiator fights.

Recruiting gladiators

51 **The first gladiators were household slaves.** The will of the dead man who was being honoured by the games would name his slaves who were to fight. They were made to fight during the funeral. Those who were killed were then buried with their owner.

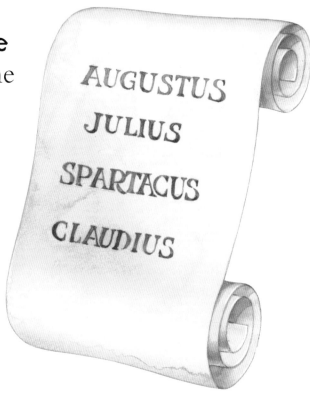

AUGUSTUS
JULIUS
SPARTACUS
CLAUDIUS

▲ Before a show, the names of the gladiators who were to fight were written on a scroll.

SPQR

CASSIUS SCRIBONIUS

CRIME
ROBBERY

SENTENCE
THREE YEARS
AS GLADIATOR

◄ When convicted, the name, crime and sentence of each criminal was inscribed on a tablet.

52 **Criminals could be sent to the arena.** The Romans did not have prisons so criminals were usually fined, flogged or executed. Men guilty of some crimes might be ordered to become gladiators for a set period of time – such as three years for robbery. These men would be given a tablet showing the details of their crime and sentence.

I DON'T BELIEVE IT!
When the lanista wanted to buy slaves to become gladiators, he would choose big, strong men. On average a gladiator was about 5 centimetres taller than an ordinary Roman.

53

Some gladiators were volunteers. These volunteers had often been former soldiers who wanted to earn money for their retirement. They signed up for a period of time or for a set number of fights and received a large payment of money if they survived.

54

Gladiators were recruited by the lanista. Every gladiator school was run by the lanista, the owner and chief trainer. The lanista decided who to recruit and how to train them. He would choose the strongest men to fight in heavy armour and the quickest men to fight as retiarius gladiators.

◄ Slaves for sale were paraded in front of potential buyers. They were sold to the highest bidder.

55

Strong slaves were sold to become gladiators. In ancient Rome, slaves were treated as the property of their owners and had no human rights at all. If a man wanted to raise money, he might sell a slave. The lanista would pay a high price for strong male slaves. Many young slaves were also sold to become gladiators.

► The price of slaves varied, but a slave might cost about the same as an average workman's wages for a year.

29

Learning to fight

56 Gladiators lived in a special training school called a ludus. Most early schools were located near Naples, but they later moved to Rome. Some schools specialized in a particular type of gladiator, but others trained all types. The school was run by the lanista, but some were owned by wealthy noblemen.

▲ Wooden training swords were the same size as real weapons.

57 Gladiators trained with wooden weapons. The weapons made sure that gladiators were not seriously injured during training. It also made it more difficult for gladiators to organize a rebellion, as Spartacus had done. Some wooden weapons were bound with heavy lead weights so that when gladiators fought with normal weapons they could fight for longer.

▲ Most arenas and gladiator schools had a small shrine dedicated to the war god Mars.

58 A special oath was taken by trainee gladiators. The sacred oath (promise) was taken in front of a shrine to the gods. The oath made the gladiator obey the lanista without question or endure branding, flogging, chains or death. Gladiators were allowed to keep any prize money they won.

Most gladiators used only one type of armour and weapon, training with them for hours every day.

59 New trainees fought against a wooden post called a palus. A trainer known as a doctor taught the recruits how to use their weapons and shields to strike at the 2 metre-high wooden post. Only when the basic tactics had been learned did the recruits practise against other gladiators.

QUIZ

1. Near which modern city were most early gladiator training schools built?
2. Why were training weapons weighed down with lead?
3. What name was given to men who trained gladiators?

Answers:
1. Naples. 2. To make them heavier and so improve the stamina of gladiators who trained with them. 3. Doctor.

▲ Gladiators trained for several hours every day, being instructed on fighting techniques by retired gladiators and more experienced men.

60 The buildings of a gladiator school were constructed around a square training ground. This was where the gladiators did most of their training, exercises and other activities. Around the training ground were rooms where the gladiators lived. Recruits slept in dormitories, but fully trained gladiators had their own rooms.

Armour, shields and helmets

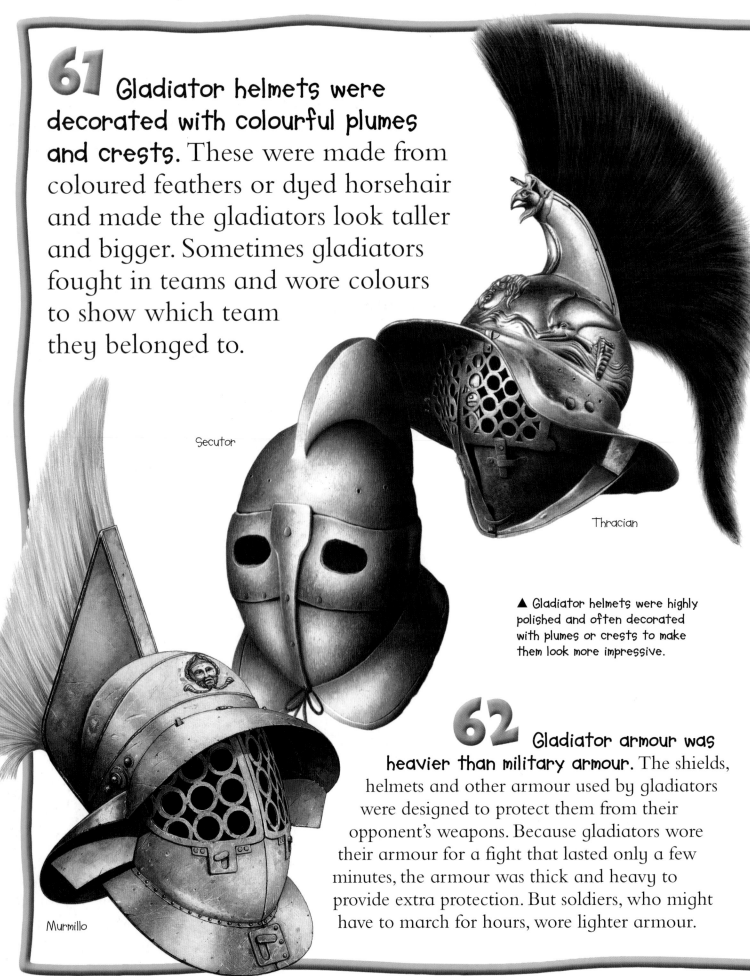

61 Gladiator helmets were decorated with colourful plumes and crests. These were made from coloured feathers or dyed horsehair and made the gladiators look taller and bigger. Sometimes gladiators fought in teams and wore colours to show which team they belonged to.

Secutor

Thracian

▲ Gladiator helmets were highly polished and often decorated with plumes or crests to make them look more impressive.

62 Gladiator armour was heavier than military armour. The shields, helmets and other armour used by gladiators were designed to protect them from their opponent's weapons. Because gladiators wore their armour for a fight that lasted only a few minutes, the armour was thick and heavy to provide extra protection. But soldiers, who might have to march for hours, wore lighter armour.

Murmillo

63 Some armour was covered with gold. Most gladiator armour was decorated with carvings and reliefs of gods such as Mars, god of war, or Victory, goddess of success. These decorations were often coated with thin sheets of pure gold.

64 Padded armour was worn on the arms and legs. Thick layers of cloth and padding gave protection from glancing blows from the weapons or from being hit by the shield of the opponent.

▲ Gladiator shields were painted and even decorated with gold to impress the audience.

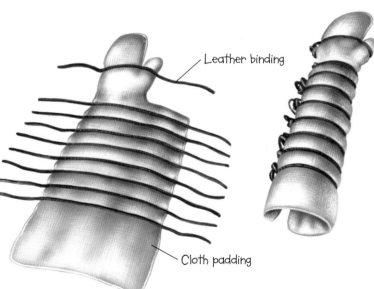

Leather binding

Cloth padding

▲ Arms and legs were often covered with layers of woollen cloth tied on with leather bindings.

65 The body was usually left without any armour at all. This meant that a single blow could kill them, or injure them so seriously that they had to ask for mercy. Gladiators needed to be skilful with both weapons and shields to survive.

I DON'T BELIEVE IT!
Gladiator helmets were very heavy – they weighed about 7 kilograms, twice as much as an army helmet!

A day in the life...

66 Gladiators were woken at dawn to begin training. They had several servants to look after them, usually boys or old men. A servant would wake the gladiator at sunrise to make sure he was ready to begin his training on time.

▲ A gladiator would be awoken at dawn by one of the slaves owned by the training school.

67 Training lasted for hours each day. Even the most experienced gladiator began his day practising weapon strokes at a wooden post. This allowed the fighter to warm up ready for the more serious training later in the day. Gladiators had special plain armour and blunt weapons to use when training.

◀ A stout wooden post about 2 metres tall was used for the more basic training exercises.

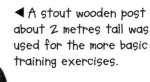

GLADIATOR MEAL

Ask an adult to help you prepare this gladiator meal

You will need:

60 g rolled porridge oats
400 ml water pinch of salt
50 g ham 5 dried figs
2 tbsp olive oil
1 tsp dried rosemary.

1. Chop the ham and figs. Fry in the olive oil and rosemary.
2. Place the oats, water and salt in a saucepan. Bring to the boil, then simmer for 5 minutes.
3. When the oats have thickened, scatter over the ham and figs.

◄ Gladiators were given simple, but nutritious food such as porridge, carrots and sausages to keep them fit and healthy.

68 Barley porridge was the usual food of gladiators, but they also ate meats, fruits and vegetables. The Romans believed that barley was a highly nutritious food that helped to build up muscles. The owner of the gladiator school did not waste money on fancy foods, but provided plain and healthy meals.

▼ Gladiators were sometimes given treatment by masseurs, doctors and other specialists who looked after their health.

69 Gladiators received regular massages. Romans knew that massages would help to ease stiff joints or relax muscles. Massages could be very helpful to old injuries. The gladiator school would employ at least one man who was an expert masseur to keep the gladiators in top condition.

70 Older, retired gladiators trained the new recruits. Gladiators who survived long enough to win their freedom often found jobs at gladiator schools. They were expert fighters and knew many tricks and special moves. They trained the new recruits to be expert fighters. This would please the crowd, and give the gladiator a better chance of surviving.

Get ready for the games

71 **The first decision was how much money to spend.** The man who staged a munus, or gladiatorial games, was known as the editor. A munus was an expensive event but most editors wanted to put on the most impressive show possible. They would spend as much money as they could spare.

72 **The editor would choose different features for his show.** A lanista would be hired to organize the show. Together, they would decide how many gladiators would fight and how many musicians and other performers were needed. The lanista would make sure the event was a success.

▲ Musicians and dancers were popular at gladiator shows. Shows often included a parade of entertainers before the gladiators appeared.

QUIZ
1. Who decided on the features for a gladiatorial show?
2. Did the editor of the games wear his everyday toga or expensive clothing?
3. Was a toga with purple edges worn by noblemen or ordinary citizens?

Answers:
1. The editor and lanista.
2. He hired special clothing to wear.
3. Noblemen.

73 **A dead gladiator cost more than a wounded one.** The editor would sign a contract with the lanista. This set down everything that would appear at the munus and the cost. If a gladiator was killed, a special payment was made so that the lanista could buy and train a replacement. Many editors granted mercy to a wounded man to avoid paying extra.

74

Everything was hired – even the clothes worn by the organizer. The editor would hire expensive clothes and jewellery for himself and his family. He wanted to make sure that they looked their best when they appeared at the games. The editor wanted to impress his fellow citizens and make sure they would vote for him.

▼ Smart clothes were hired for the editor and all his family so that they could show off to the audience.

75

The star of the show was the editor. Everything was arranged so that the editor of the games looked as important as possible. As well as wearing special clothes, he was given the most prominent seat in the amphitheatre and all the gladiators and other performers bowed to him. He was paying for the show and wanted to make sure he got all the credit.

A laurel wreath signified an honour granted by the Roman government

Gold jewellery indicated a family's wealth

Brightly coloured silk from China showed wealth and sophistication

Purple was the most expensive dye in ancient Rome

A toga was a special item of clothing that indicated the rank within society of the man wearing it

Showtime!

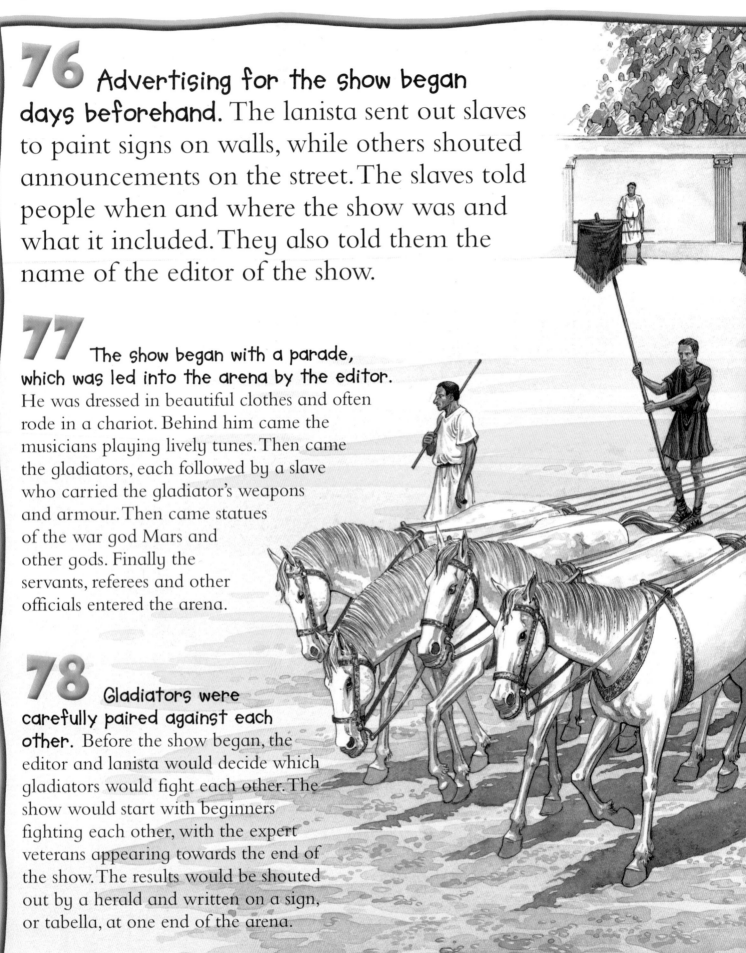

76 **Advertising for the show began days beforehand.** The lanista sent out slaves to paint signs on walls, while others shouted announcements on the street. The slaves told people when and where the show was and what it included. They also told them the name of the editor of the show.

77 **The show began with a parade, which was led into the arena by the editor.** He was dressed in beautiful clothes and often rode in a chariot. Behind him came the musicians playing lively tunes. Then came the gladiators, each followed by a slave who carried the gladiator's weapons and armour. Then came statues of the war god Mars and other gods. Finally the servants, referees and other officials entered the arena.

78 **Gladiators were carefully paired against each other.** Before the show began, the editor and lanista would decide which gladiators would fight each other. The show would start with beginners fighting each other, with the expert veterans appearing towards the end of the show. The results would be shouted out by a herald and written on a sign, or tabella, at one end of the arena.

79 **The probatio was a crucial ceremony.** Before the first fight of the show, the editor and lanista would enter the arena for the probatio. This ceremony involved the men testing the weapons and armour to be used in the show. Swords were tested by slicing up vegetables, and armour by being hit with clubs.

◀ Each gladiator show began with a grand parade of everyone involved in the show, led by the editor in a chariot.

80 **Musicians performed first.** The band included trumpets, curved horns and the hydraulis. This was a loud instrument like a modern church organ. The musicians entertained the crowd between fights and played music during the show ceremonies.

TRUE OR FALSE?

1. The hydraulis was an instrument like a modern trumpet.
2. Weapons were tested before the show to make sure they were sharp.
3. Gladiators wore their armour during the opening parade.

Answers:
1. FALSE The hydraulis was an instrument like a modern organ. 2. TRUE Weapons were tested during the probatio ceremony. 3. FALSE Slaves carried the armour behind the gladiators.

Water fights

81 Some gladiatorial shows took place on water. The most impressive of all were the naumachiae, or sea fights. For these shows, an artificial lake 557 metres long by 536 metres wide was dug beside the river Tiber. Small warships were brought up the river and launched on the lake when a sea fight was due to take place.

82 Naval fights were recreations of real battles. In 2BC, Emperor Augustus staged a naumachia that recreated a battle fought 400 years earlier between the Greeks and the Persians. Emperor Titus staged a battle that originally started between the Greeks and Egyptians. These battles did not always end with the same winner as the real battle.

▼ Recreated naval battles were extremely expensive to stage, so didn't take place very often.

In AD84, a storm drenched the audience during
a naumachia – nearly everyone caught a cold.

83
The first naval gladiators did not try to kill each other. The first of the sea battles were staged by Julius Caesar to celebrate a naval victory. The show was designed to impress the audience with the skills of the sailors and the way Caesar had won his victory.

85
One naval show involved 19,000 men. Emperor Claudius staged a sea battle on Lake Fucino. The men fighting were not sailors or gladiators but criminals condemned to death. Most of the men died and any survivors were sent to work as slaves.

84
The Colosseum in Rome could be flooded for naval fights. When the Colosseum was first built it had special pipes that could fill the arena with water and then drain it away again. The flooded arena was used for fights between special miniature warships crewed by gladiators. Later, the pipes were replaced by trapdoors and stage scenery.

I DON'T BELIEVE IT!

On one occasion, gladiators took one look at the poor condition of the warships and refused to board them.

41

Wild animal hunts

86 The first wild animal show was to celebrate a military victory. In 164BC Rome defeated the powerful North African city of Carthage. The victorious general, Publius Cornelius Scipio, was given the nickname Africanus. He brought back to Rome hundreds of African wild animals, such as elephants, crocodiles and lions. After parading the animals through the streets, he included them in his gladiatorial games.

▲ This ancient mosaic shows the capture of wild animals, such as lions and gazelles. They were then shipped to Rome to fight in the arenas.

87 One elephant hunt went badly wrong. In 79BC General Gnaeus Pompey staged a wild elephant hunt with 20 elephants in a temporary arena in Rome. The crowd was protected by a tall iron fence, but two of the elephants charged at the fence, smashing it down. The elephants were quickly killed by hunters, but several people were injured.

88 The design of the arena changed to make it safer for the crowds. As the wild animal shows became more popular the need to keep the watching crowd safe meant changes to the arena had to be made. The arena was sunk about 3 metres into the ground and surrounded by a vertical wall of smooth stone. No animal could leap up the wall or break it down, so the spectators were safe from attack.

89

Some animal shows were fantastic and strange. The Romans loved to see animals fighting each other. Sometimes a group of lions or wolves would be set to attack zebras or deer. At other times two hunting animals would be made to fight each other. They were often chained together to encourage them to fight. Some pairings were very odd. A snake was set against a lion, a seal set to fight a wolf or a bull against a bear.

90

Lions were set to fight tigers. One of the most popular animal fights was when a lion was set against a tiger. So many lions and tigers were sent to Rome to die in the fights that they became extinct in some areas of North Africa and the Middle East.

I DON'T BELIEVE IT!

The Romans loved watching animals that had been trained to perform tricks. One animal trainer put on shows in which an ape drove a chariot pulled by camels.

▼ A wild tiger attacks a gladiator, as seen in the 2000 movie *Gladiator*. Wild animals were part of most arena shows.

Outside Rome

91 More gladiators fought in southern Italy than in Rome. The idea of gladiatorial fights came from Campania, the area of Italy around Naples. For hundreds of years, the gladiator schools in Campania produced the best-trained gladiators and had more than anywhere else. One school had over 5000 gladiators training at one time.

92 The city of London had a small arena for gladiatorial games and other events. It stood inside the city walls beside the army fortress, near what is now St Paul's Cathedral. The 30-metre-long amphitheatre was built of stone and timber and could seat around 4000 spectators. St Albans, Chester and Caerleon also had amphitheatres.

▼ The arena at Pompeii. The oval shape, banked seating and two exits were the common design for all arenas.

93

All gladiatorial shows had to honour the emperor. By about AD50, political power was in the hands of the emperor. It was the emperor who decided who could stand for election, and who would win the election. The editor of a gladiator show always began by dedicating the show to the emperor.

▶ A statue of an emperor. Such a statue stood in most arenas and other public buildings.

94

The best gladiators were sent to Rome. Gladiators who fought in provinces such as Britain or Spain were owned by lanistas who travelled from city to city to put on a show. Agents from Rome would watch these shows and any gladiator who was particularly good would be taken to Rome to fight in the the Colosseum.

▼ A gladiator fight reaches its end, as seen in the 1960 movie *Spartacus*.

95

Some towns banned gladiators. Not everyone enjoyed the fights. Many Romans refused to attend the games. Some cities, particularly in Greece and the eastern provinces, did not have an amphitheatre and refused to put on combats. Some people thought the fights were a waste of good slaves.

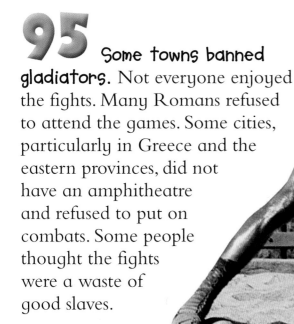

The last gladiators

▲ A scene from the 2000 movie *Gladiator*. The bloodshed in gladiator fights appalled some Romans.

96 Gladiatorial games became less and less popular. Seneca, a wise man and a great thinker, wrote that attending the games made Romans more cruel and inhuman than they had been before. The writer Artemidorus of Daldis said that the games were dishonourable, cruel and wicked. However most Romans approved of the games and enjoyed watching them.

97 In AD324, Christian bishops tried to ban gladiatorial fights. After AD250, Christianity became popular in the Roman Empire. Christians believed that the fights were sinful and they asked Emperor Constantine I to ban the fights. He banned private games, but allowed state games to continue.

QUIZ

1. Which philosopher thought watching gladiator fights made people cruel?
2. Which emperor closed down the gladiator schools in Rome?
3. Which emperor banned private gladiatorial games?

Answers:
1. Seneca. 2. Emperor Honorius.
3. Emperor Constantine I.

98

In AD366 Pope Damasus used gladiators to murder rival churchmen. When Pope Liberius died the cardinals of Rome could not agree on a successor. Followers who wanted Ursinus to be the next pope were meeting in the church of St Maria Trastevere when Damasus hired a gang of gladiators to attack them. The gladiators broke into the church and killed 137 people. Damasus then became pope.

99

The Christian monk Telemachus was the first to stop a gladiator fight. During a show in the Colosseum in AD404, Telemachus forced apart two fighting gladiators. He made a speech asking for the shows to stop, but angry spectators killed him. Emperor Honorius then closed down all the gladiator schools in Rome.

▲ Heavily armed gladiators were sometimes hired by ambitious politicians and churchmen to murder their rivals.

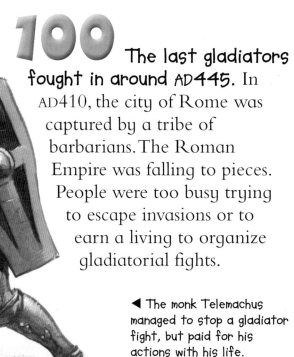

100

The last gladiators fought in around AD445. In AD410, the city of Rome was captured by a tribe of barbarians. The Roman Empire was falling to pieces. People were too busy trying to escape invasions or to earn a living to organize gladiatorial fights.

◄ The monk Telemachus managed to stop a gladiator fight, but paid for his actions with his life.

Index